PRAYER BREATHS

100 Days of Prayer Power, As Close As Your Next Breath

Bishop George W. Brooks
Lady Edna Brooks & Keva Brooks Napper

PRAYER BREATHS
100 DAYS OF PRAYER POWER, AS CLOSE AS YOUR NEXT BREATH

Published by Lee's Press and Publishing Company
2618 Battleground Ave
STE A #233
Greensboro NC 27408

All rights reserved, Except for brief excerpts for review purposes, no part of this book may be reproduced or used in any form without written permission from MEEK Legacy, LLC and/or the publisher.

This document is published by Lee's Press and Publishing Company located in the United States of America. It is protected by the United States Copyright Act, all applicable state laws and international copyright laws. The information in this document is accurate to the best of the ability of MEEK Legacy, LLC at the time of writing. The content of this document is subject to change without notice.

ISBN-13: 978-0692634844 *Paperback*
ISBN-10: 0692634843

Library of Congress Cataloging-in-Publication Data

TABLE OF CONTENTS

Dedication 6

Acknowledgements 8

Introduction 10

Day 1: Maintaining Authority 12

Day 2: Spirit of Supplication 13

Day 3: Guidance 14

Day 4: To Follow After God 15

Day 5: Inner Healing 16

Day 6: Guidance and Direction 17

Day 7: His Presence 18

Day 8: Hear My Cry 19

Day 9: Confidence in God 20

Day 10: Individual Strength 21

Day 11: Peace of God 22

Day 12: Rest in God 23

Day 13: God's Strength 24

Day 14: His Faithfulness 25

Day 15: Strength for Change 26

Day 16: Rest For My Soul 27

Day 17: Hope in the Future 28

Day 18: Sweet Sleep 29

Day 19: Renewed Strength 30
Day 20: Peace and Strength 31
Day 21: A Load of Benefits 32
Day 22: New Mercies 33
Day 23: Bless the Lord 34
Day 24: God's Love 35
Day 25: Salvation 36
Day 26: God's Love 37
Day 27: Hear the Voice of God 38
Day 28: Unity 39
Day 29: Contentment 40
Day 30: Search and Cleanse Me 41
Day 31: Trust in God 42
Day 32: The Fruit of My Lips 43
Day 33: My Physical Body 44
Day 34: A Well Balanced Life 45
Day 35: Protection 46
Day 36: Misunderstood Pain 47
Day 37: Encouraged 48
Day 38: Resourcefulness 49
Day 39: Peace 50
Day 40: In the Box 51
Day 41: Safe and Peaceful 52

Day 42: A Hiding Place 53
Day 43: It's a Race 54
Day 44: Timely Victory 55
Day 45: Almost Exhausted 56
Day 46: Delighted in God 57
Day 47: Curves in the Road 58
Day 48: Green Pasture 59
Day 49: Putting on New Garments 60
Day 50: Unity 61
Day 51: Financial Stewardship 62
Day 52: Help From the Lord 63
Day 53: A Loving God 64
Day 54: Family 65
Day 55: Thankful 66
Day 56: My Image 67
Day 57: Family 68
Day 58: Protection 69
Day 59: Protection 70
Day 60: Protection 71
Day 61: Fear 72
Day 62: Fear 73
Day 63: Fear 74
Day 64: Strength 75

Day 65: Peace 76
Day 66: Victory 77
Day 67: Faith for the Future 78
Day 68: A Proper View of God 79
Day 69: I Cannot Grow Stronger by Myself 80
Day 70: Overcoming Being Wounded 81
Day 71: Finding a Large Miracle in a Small Situation ..82
Day 72: Sharing 83
Day 73: Understanding 84
Day 74: Knowing God Really Cares 85
Day 75: Being a Servant for the KING 86
Day 76: Universal Beauty 87
Day 77: How I Overcame 88
Day 78: Today 89
Day 79: Family 90
Day 80: Family 91
Day 81: Family 92
Day 82: Death 93
Day 83: No Condemnation 94
Day 84: Deliverance 95
Day 85: Bad News 96
Day 86: Prejudice 97
Day 87: My Thoughts 98

Day 88: The Word 99
Day 89: Guarding My Mouth 100
Day 90: Affliction 101
Day 91: Being Diverted 102
Day 92: Being Diverted 103
Day 93: Status 104
Day 94: Maturity 105
Day 95: Power 106
Day 96: Victorious 107
Day 97: My Steps 108
Day 98: My Insurance 109
Day 99: Maturing 110
Day 100: My Final Resolve 111
About The Authors 112

DEDICATION

Bishop George W. Brooks

To my deceased grandparents, Deacon Tom and Nancy Watkins who were feverent prayer warriors.

To my deceased grandparents, Pastor Joe and Lydia Brooks, who practiced prayer in their daily life.

To my parents, the late Pastor Luther A. Brooks and Mary Catherine Brooks, who taught us not only to believe in prayer, but to believe in the God to whom we were praying.

Lady Edna Brooks

To my deceased parents, Deacon Willie (Bill) and Cyrilla Graves.

To my Father who believed that God could heal me when I was diagnosed with a brain tumor at the age of eight. God answered his prayers.

To my mother who taught me that prayer was more powerful than trying to change things in the flesh.

To all the women who have partnered with me over the years to do warfare to tear down strongholds.

Keva Brooks Napper

To my uncle, the late Vance Carlacy Brooks who always encouraged me to stay on the straight and narrow.

To the families of Zion who took me in from birth and fed me, kept me, made me do homework and my Sunday school lessons! If I didn't know my scriptures, or the hymn to play for Sunday morning I couldn't go outside and play! Thank you for your accountability and making sure the word was in me, not just around me.

ACKNOWLEDGEMENTS

Thanks to Kevin, Kim, Calvin, Jocelyn, Kiandra, Keyon, Gavin, Kaleb for standing with us in all situations.

Thanks to our family for your consistent support.

Thanks to Mount Zion Baptist Church of Greensboro, Inc. where we pastored for 37 years and learned so much about the power of prayer.

Thanks to Pastor Bryan and Lady Debra Pierce for leading Mount Zion with much emphasis on prayer.

Thanks to my pastor, Bishop Neil C. Ellis, who is helping to resurrect the dying discipline of prayer through Global United Fellowship.

Thanks to Pastor Samuel Otu Pimpong and the Legon Baptist Church in Ghana, West Africa for saturating the heavens with constant prayer and intercession.

Thanks to the House of Elijah and The Elijah Project for helping to hone and refine our walk with God through prayer and supplication.

Thanks to our prayer partners and groups who have held us up throughout the years.

Thank you to Joy Cook and Joy Cook Public Relations Group.

INTRODUCTION

We have a command from God to pray without ceasing. In other words, we are to never stop praying. Did God really mean to pray always? Is that really possible?

We often agree with the word but then ignore it in our everyday living. Often times that's because we lack understanding of how to incorporate that word into our daily circumstances. It's impossible to talk to God non-stop all day long. But God would not require us to do anything we could not possibly do. So what does pray without ceasing really mean? I believe it means being continuously aware that God is with us always and is involved in our everyday affairs. Therefore, we should have a constant dependence on God in everything we do, whether it's everyday chores or a challenging situation.

Jesus, in his parables, often used something natural to explain something spiritual. Praying without ceasing or whispering prayers all throughout the day is like breathing. Let's call this spiritual breathing.

Breathing is not something we have to think about, it comes naturally. On the other hand, holding our breath is much more difficult and can cause some serious problems if held too long. When we don't pray, we are holding our spiritual breath and can cause some serious problems if held too long. Breathing may come easily but praying will not unless it's intentional.

This book is designed to promote and encourage praying without ceasing by intentionally making prayer quick and easy, like breathing. Let's take some PRAYER BREATHS in the WORD of GOD!

DAY 1

Prayer Focus: Maintaining Authority
Scripture Focus: Genesis 1:26

Father, I thank you for giving me dominion over all that You have created. By Your power, I am well able to daily walk in my God-given authority and not fall prey to anything the enemy has planned for my downfall. In the name of Jesus I pray.

Confession: God's authority makes me more than a conqueror in all things.

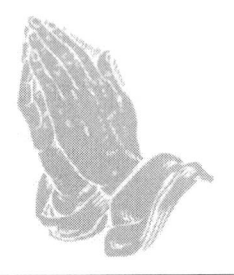

DAY 2

Prayer Focus: Spirit of Supplication
Scripture Focus: Philippians 4:6-7

Lord give me a praying spirit. Let a spirit of supplication rest upon me so that I may experience a peace that guards me from nagging anxiety. Thank You that I live in the power of peace. In the name of Jesus. Amen.

Confession: My prayer disrupts the plans of the enemy.

DAY 3

Prayer Focus: Guidance
Scripture Focus: 2 Samuel 22:29

Lord, I thank you that when I can't see my way I can depend on You to guide me, You light my path. Thank You for watching over me and guiding me along the best pathway for my life. In the name of Jesus I pray.

Confession: I can depend on God to show me the way I should go.

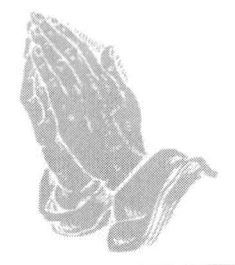

<u>DAY 4</u>

Prayer Focus: To Follow After God
Scripture Focus: Psalm 63:8

Father, I purpose to be in hot pursuit of you. You are my top priority. By the power of the Holy Spirit I will not allow the concerns of this day to move you out of Your Lordship over me. Master, I cling to you with my whole being. In the name of Jesus I pray.

Confession: I am in hot pursuit of God.

DAY 5

Prayer Focus: Inner Healing
Scripture Focus: Psalm 23:3

Lord, you are my shepherd and the keeper of my soul. I cast every care on you and I forgive and release every person who has wounded me. Help me, Father, to walk in love and forgiveness: healing begins with forgiveness. In the name of Jesus I pray, amen.

Confession: I will not tolerate an unforgiving spirit in my heart.

<u>DAY 6</u>

Prayer Focus: Guidance and Direction
Scripture Focus: Deuteronomy 30:9-10

Heavenly Father, for being a God of order and instruction, I give you thanks. As I start my day, I ask that you guide, direct and protect me and help me to succeed in everything I do. In the name of Jesus I pray.

Confession: God will give me divine wisdom to make right decisions today.

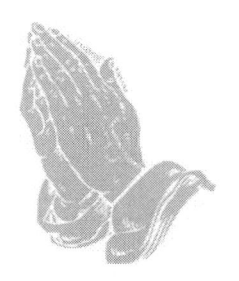

DAY 7

Prayer Focus: His Presence
Scripture Focus: Psalm 16:8, 11

May I always sense your very presence and your loving arms of protection around me. As you manifest your glory my heart is made glad and I am full of your joy. In the name of Jesus I pray.

Confession: The Lord is always with me, therefore, I will not be shaken.

DAY 8

Prayer Focus: Hear My Cry
Scripture Focus: Psalm 61: 1-2

Father, I come boldly to you making my petitions known. I ask you to move on my behalf making every crooked place straight and every empty place full of your peace. You are my refuge and strength and I trust You that all my needs will be supplied.

Confession: When I am overwhelmed I will run to the Rock.

DAY 9

Prayer Focus: Confidence in God
Scripture Focus: Hebrews 3:14

Almighty God, create in me a clean heart and renew a right spirit within me. Help me to boldly hold on to my confidence and remain faithful until the end.

Confession: The Lord is my refuge and strength, He will keep me from falling.

DAY 10

Prayer Focus: Individual Strength
Scripture Focus: Galatians 6:9

Father God, I thank you for the strength to wait and not give up. You are my strength, therefore, I will not lose heart, grow weary and faint, but I will wait for my due season. In the name of Jesus I pray.

Confession: I will not grow weary of well doing and I will reap a harvest in due season.

DAY 11

Prayer Focus: Peace of God
Scripture Focus: Ephesians 6:23; Philippians 4:7

Precious Father, I come boldly before your throne asking for peace that only you can give. Let it be a peace so powerful that it will guard my heart and mind through Christ Jesus. Thank you for peace that is greater than my understanding.

Confession: I am full of peace that only God can give.

DAY 12

Prayer Focus: Rest in God
Scripture Focus: Matthew 11:28

Lord God, you are well able to deliver me from unrealistic expectations and heavy burdens. I cast all my cares on you and in You I find rest for my soul. In the name of Jesus I pray.

Confession: I am free from heavy burdens.

DAY 13

Prayer Focus: God's Strength
Scripture Focus: Joel 3:10; II Corinthians 12:9

Precious Father, when I am challenged with trials and tests in life, your strength is enough for me. In my weakness your power is made perfect, therefore when I am weak then I am strong. In Jesus name I pray.

Confession: Because of Christ, when I am weak I can declare I am strong.

DAY 14

Prayer Focus: His Faithfulness
Scripture Focus: Hebrews 13:5

Father, I am so thankful that you are always there for me. I can never disappoint you so much that you will walk away from me. I am so grateful for your faithfulness. Thank you that your faithfulness is GREAT!
In the name of Jesus I pray.

Confession: I can trust God to have my back.

DAY 15

Prayer Focus: Strength for Change
Scripture Focus: Daniel 2:21

Dear God, I know that change is inevitable, but when it comes, help me to be positive and productive with each new phase of my life. Help me to resist the urge to run. May the changes I'm facing shake up my courage and strength in You.

Confession: I will embrace positive change for me.

DAY 16

Prayer Focus: Rest For My Soul
Scripture Focus: Psalm 116:7

When I feel restless and overwhelmed because of the challenges in my life, help me to remember You have been so good to me. You are my Keeper and my Provider, Thank You.

Confession: I will rest in the Lord regardless.

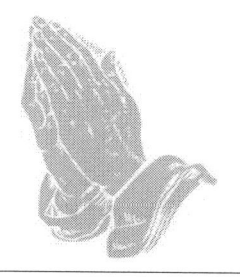

DAY 17

Prayer Focus: Hope in the Future
Scripture Focus: Jeremiah 31:17

Lord I Thank you that there will always be hope in my future. No circumstance can destroy my hope because my hope is in You.

Confession: I will always have HOPE.

DAY 18

Prayer Focus: Sweet Sleep
Scripture Focus: Psalm 4:8

Father, so many distractions come to steal my peace and prevent me from resting well throughout the night. But I will lie down in peace and have sweet sleep because You will keep me safe.

Confession: I expect to have sweet sleep every night.

DAY 19

Prayer Focus: Renewed Strength
Scripture Focus: Psalm 103:5

Thank You Lord that You renew my strength when I feel weak and powerless. Your strength is a powerful force that can withstand any challenge the enemy brings against me.

Confession: God is the key to my strength.

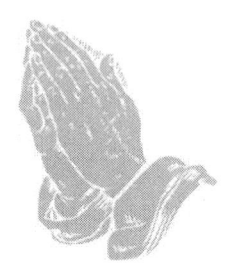

DAY 20

Prayer Focus: Peace and Strength
Scripture Focus: Psalm 29:11

Heavenly Father, You know about all my circumstances and all my trials. Thank You that You will give me strength and bless me with peace so that I can overcome them all.

Confession: God's peace gives me strength.

DAY 21

Prayer Focus: A Load of Benefits
Scripture Focus: Psalm 68:19

Almighty God, thank You that I begin each new day with a load of benefits. There is no one that can bless me the way You do.

Confession: I am daily loaded with benefits.

DAY 22

Prayer Focus: New Mercies
Scripture Focus: Lamentations 3:22-23

Heavenly Father, because you supply me with new mercies every morning, problems are powerless to consume me. I will not be defeated because your compassion will never fail. Thank You that your faithfulness is so great.

Confession: With each new day, I get new mercies.

DAY 23

Prayer Focus: Bless the Lord
Scripture Focus: Psalm 103:1

Heavenly Father, I choose to bless you today. I command every part of me to bless your Holy Name.

Confession: Blessings will always be in my mouth for God.

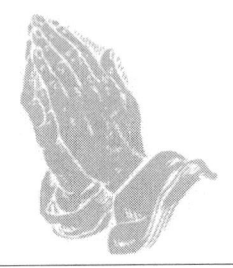

DAY 24

Prayer Focus: God's Love
Scripture Focus: Romans 5:8

Heavenly Father, it is truly awesome to me that while I was still living in sin, Christ died for me. What a mighty demonstration of your love.

Confession: God's love is beyond comprehension.

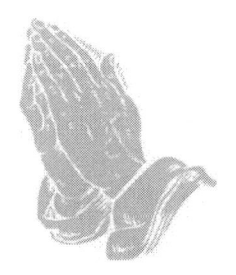

DAY 25

Prayer Focus: Salvation
Scripture Focus: John 3:16

Father God, Thank You that You loved me so much that You gave your only Son to pay the price for my sins. Because I believe in Him, I have eternal life.

Confession: I have eternal life through Jesus.

DAY 26

Prayer Focus: God's Love
Scripture Focus: John 15:9

Heavenly Father, I ask for a deeper revelation of your love so I can better understand how to dwell in it. I want to be consumed by your love.

Confession: An intimate relationship with God is my goal.

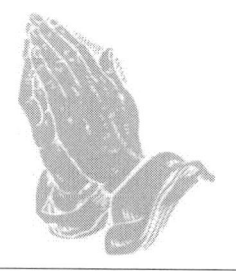

DAY 27

Prayer Focus: Hear the Voice of God
Scripture Focus: Psalm 46:10

Dear God, release your strong, holy, warring angels over my life and the lives of those connected to me to guard, protect and fight in battle for us! I will be still, with a quieted soul, so that I may hear from you.

Confession: I am listening for the voice of God.

DAY 28

Prayer Focus: Unity
Scripture Focus: Nehemiah 4:19-20

Dear God, in these perilous times, help me to rebuild the wall of unity that was torn down by the divisive facets of the world.

Confession: I will unite not untie.

DAY 29

Prayer Focus: Contentment
Scripture Focus: Philippians 4:6-7,11,19

Lord, show me your definition of contentment and let worry not invade my life in Jesus name and for Your glory.

Confession: Whatever is of God, is contentment for me.

DAY 30

Prayer Focus: Search and Cleanse Me
Scripture Focus: Psalm 139: 23-24

Lord, show me as I am. You know me better than I know myself. Search my heart and clean me up.

Confession: I desire correction for growth.

DAY 31

Prayer Focus: Trust in God
Scripture Focus: 1 Corinthians 1:9

God, how wonderful you are to remove me from a superficial selfishness to a substantial and meaningful relationship with you that I can depend on.

Confession: I only deceive myself when everything is about me and not about God.

DAY 32

Prayer Focus: The Fruit of My Lips
Scripture Focus: Proverbs 18:21

Father, I pray that you will be pleased with the fruit of my lips. I pray that my tongue will be a ready writing pen and when I speak it will bring life.

Confession: My tongue is either deadly or death defying.

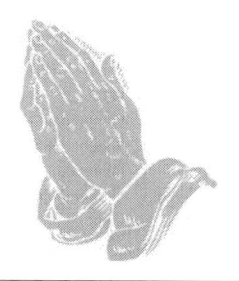

DAY 33

Prayer Focus: My Physical Body
Scripture Focus: 1 Corinthians 6:19-20

Lord, since my body is not my own, but your dwelling place, teach me through my eating habits and exercise how to be a good steward over it.

Confession: God lives in me.

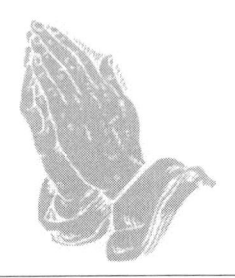

DAY 34

Prayer Focus: A Well Balanced Life
Scripture Focus: Proverbs 11:1-3

Lord, direct me from extremes so that I neither misrepresent you nor deny your power. Help me stay balanced.

Confession: God's choice is my choice.

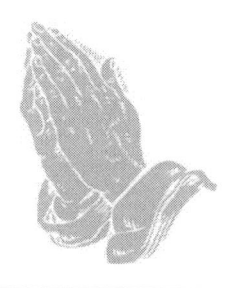

DAY 35

Prayer Focus: Protection
Scripture Focus: Psalm 18:2

Ever vigilant Father, as a roof provides a covering for a building, continue to provide a covering from my adversaries for my body, soul and spirit in Jesus name I pray.

Confession: God provides 24/7 protection.

DAY 36

Prayer Focus: Misunderstood Pain
Scripture Focus: Psalm 138:8

My loving God, the full depth and the intensity of the pain exceeds my limited threshold but falls well within your power to heal and deliver. Please grant me your ultimate plan so I applaud your infinite wisdom.

Confession: Even if I don't understand, God is still in charge.

DAY 37

Prayer Focus: Encouraged
Scripture Focus: Psalm 138:3

God you are wonderful, you enabled me to move past the stiff joints, the unsightly rash, the disabling pain, the debilitating symptoms and the side effects of the medicines to see the sunset and the culmination of another day. Thank you for the possibility of a tomorrow.

Confession: God your presence overrides my side effects of life.

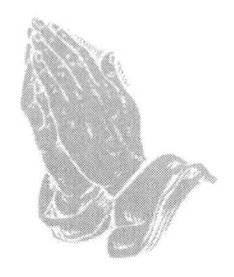

DAY 38

Prayer Focus: Resourcefulness
Scripture Focus: Psalm 138:8

Dear Lord, Thank you for adding human resources while seeking divine healing. The medical team did not remove the source of this illness but offered a different perspective on how to be involved in a victory parade rather than a defeating processional.

Confession: God is using what's available.

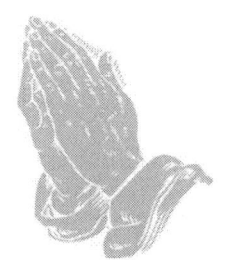

DAY 39

Prayer Focus: Peace
Scripture Focus: Numbers 6:26

Lord of the Angel Armies,
Let my life be a witness to the fact that in the midst of the most chaotic and confusing times, you are the one stable power that can and will transform my environment into a place of tranquility because of your peace.

Confession: The requirement for God's peace is His presence.

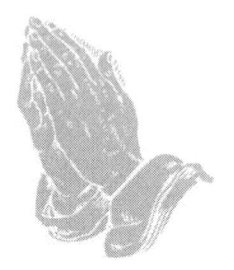

DAY 40

Prayer Focus: In the Box
Scripture Focus: Psalm 139:5

Lord, it seems that the four walls are closing in on me. I was going to give up until I realized that you had placed these walls around me so that I could see that it was your hands protecting me. You never cease to amaze me with your love for me.

Confession: A box can be protection or a prison.

DAY 41

Prayer Focus: Safe and Peaceful
Scripture Focus: Psalm 4:8

Lord, sometimes it seems there is no place to be safe and secure. Even in my sleep, nightmares can run rampant in my mind. But in you I find sweet sleep and know that I am safe in your arms.

Confession: My safety is never compromised in Christ.

DAY 42

Prayer Focus: A Hiding Place
Scripture Focus: Psalm 16:1

My strong tower Jesus, raging storms, billowing oppositions, waves of disappointment, tattering lies and crushing situations cannot keep you from me nor me from you! You are my refuge and hiding palace.

Confession: God has been a shelter for me.

DAY 43

Prayer Focus: It's a Race
Scripture Focus: Acts 20:24

Father in heaven, I pray to finish strong in this race. This will enable me to complete your assignment for my life and glorify your Name. Thank you for the assignment.

Confession: I must finish the race no matter the position.

DAY 44

Prayer Focus: Timely Victory
Scripture Focus: Psalm 60:12

Long suffering Jesus, with outstretched arms, exhausted body and a renewed mind, my prayer leads me to be a voluntary victim of God's love and will not stop until it has captured and embraced me from my head to the soles of my feet.

Confession: It is my choice to be in the Army of the Lord.

DAY 45

Prayer Focus: Almost Exhausted
Scripture Focus: Revelation 3:2

My Rose of Sharon, I have been fighting for endless days and nights. I have called on your name and relief still is a stranger at my door. Lord, empower me until I am again motivated to dream and expect promotion.

Confession: My fight is not futile.

DAY 46

Prayer Focus: Delighting in God
Scripture Focus: Psalm 37:23

Wonderful Master, my footsteps were unstable until I surrendered to your will and your way. Thank you for your stabilizing hand of mercy and your supporting arm of grace.

Confession: Stability is of God.

DAY 47

Prayer Focus: Curves in the Road
Scripture Focus: Luke 3:5

Mountain moving Jesus, You make my curved roads straight; my mountains you make into small ant hills; my valleys are made level and my decaying life is being transformed into a vibrant testimony of your goodness.

Confession: Curves in the road are not a problem for our Creator.

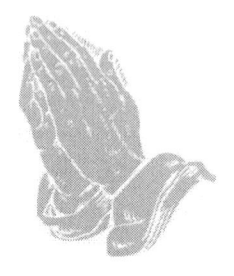

DAY 48

Prayer Focus: Green Pastures
Scripture Focus: John 10:3

Great Shepherd, I was enclosed in the pasture of negative thoughts and locked in the barrenness of nothing. I kept walking in a circle until you opened the gate and I escaped to the blessed meadows of your loving directions. Bless your wonderful leadership.

Confession: God leads, I follow without question.

DAY 49

Prayer Focus: Putting on New Garments
Scripture Focus: Ephesians 6:10-18. John 14:13-14

My Commander and General, I make a commitment today to change the way I dress. I am putting on every piece of the fighting armor that you left for me. As you train me daily, I win for the Kingdom.

Confession: The new garments of God are my protection.

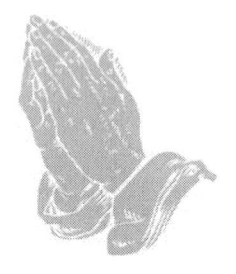

DAY 50

Prayer Focus: Unity
Scripture Focus: Ephesians 4:3

God, help me to desire to walk in unity towards my brothers and sisters, not only in words but in deeds also. When I speak, I pray for words that build others up and not tear them down.

Confession: I am my brother's keeper.

DAY 51

Prayer Focus: Financial Stewardship
Scripture Focus: Luke 6:38

Father, help me to be a good steward of the financial resources You have entrusted to me. Guide me through all my expenditures, investments and gifts to advance Your kingdom and meet the needs of others for your glory. Amen

Confession: My financial success is God's will for my life.

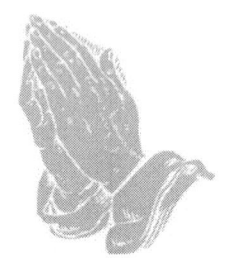

DAY 52

Prayer Focus: Help From the Lord
Scripture Focus: Psalm 118:6

Father, I confess I need your help. If you do not help me there is no other help for me. I am not smart enough to take care of me; therefore, I trust you with every area of my life. I am totally dependent upon You for my every need, even those needs that I am unaware of. In the name of Jesus, Amen.

Confession: God is active in every segment of my life.

DAY 53

Prayer Focus: A Loving God
Scripture Focus: Mark 12:30-31

Father, I thank you for loving me with an everlasting love. Daily You look beyond my faults and see the need I have for Your no strings attached unconditional love. Teach me how to love those whom it may be difficult for me to love.

Confession: God's love is not designed just for me but others as well.

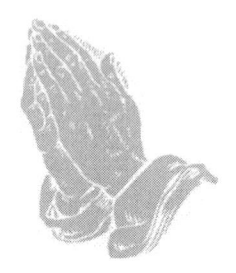

DAY 54

Prayer Focus: Family
Scripture Focus: Joshua 24:15

Lord, I come before you making petitions and intercession for my household. I declare You are the living God over our lives and I plead the blood of Jesus over my family.

Confession: My family is important to me and God.

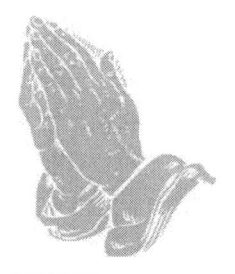

DAY 55

Prayer Focus: Thankful
Scripture Focus: 1 Chronicles 16:34

Dear God, We are thankful for your grace, your mercy, your faithfulness, your kindness, your goodness, your healing virtue, your delivering power, your saving power and for being the GREAT I AM………………

Confession: God is…………………..

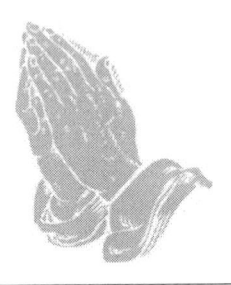

DAY 56

Prayer Focus: My Image
Scripture Focus: Psalm. 139:14

Heavenly Father, no matter what others may think of me and no matter what I have been through, I can truly say I am fearfully and wonderfully made. Your work in my life is simply marvelous. In the name of Jesus I pray.

Confession: I am unique and special, there is no one else exactly like me.

DAY 57

Prayer Focus: Family
Scripture Focus: Galatians 3:13

Mighty God, I am thankful that my family is redeemed from the curse of the law. By the blood of Jesus we are redeemed from poverty, sickness and all manner of bondages. Nothing is too hard for you! In the name of Jesus I pray.

Confession: The enemy cannot destroy my family.

DAY 58

Prayer Focus: Protection
Scripture Focus: Job 1:10

Almighty God, I pray for a hedge of protection around my body, mind, family, finances and all my possessions. Because of you I will dwell in safety. In the name of Jesus I pray.

Confession: I am surrounded with a hedge of protection.

DAY 59

Prayer Focus: Protection
Scripture Focus: Psalm 91:11-12

Heavenly Father, I thank you that you have assigned angels to guard and protect us through seen and unseen danger. They assist us with hard circumstances and walk with us through whatever issues we are facing. Thank you for loving us so! In the name of Jesus I pray.

Confession: Angels watch over me day and night.

DAY 60

Prayer Focus: Protection
Scripture Focus: Psalm 17:8

Precious Father, Thank You for making me the apple of your eye. You hide me under the shadow of your wings, therefore I am kept safe from destruction. In the name of Jesus I pray.

Confession: I am the apple of God's eye.

DAY 61

Prayer Focus: Fear
Scripture Focus: Zephaniah 3:17

Father, you quiet my emotions when fear is raging. Thank You for your strength and power that renders fear powerless to succeed. In the name of Jesus I pray.

Confession: Fear has no power over me.

DAY 62

Prayer Focus: Fear
Scripture Focus: I John 4:18

Heavenly Father, I come boldly to Your throne declaring that I will not be tormented with fear because Your perfect love cast out fear. By Your power and love I reject fear every time it comes. In the name of Jesus I pray.

Confession: God's love gives me the power to reject fear.

DAY 63

Prayer Focus: Fear
Scripture Focus: 2 Timothy 1:7

Father God, Thank You for the knowledge that you have not given me a spirit of fear, but You have given me power, love and a sound mind. Therefore I will not tolerate fear. In the name of Jesus I pray.

Confession: I will beat down fear with the word of God.

DAY 64

Prayer Focus: Strength
Scripture Focus: Psalms 29:11

Heavenly Father, Thank You for strength that is strong enough to withstand every attack of the enemy. I am so grateful that I don't have to depend on my strength because your strength is unshakeable.

Confession: I am never without the strength I need. God arms me with unshakeable strength.

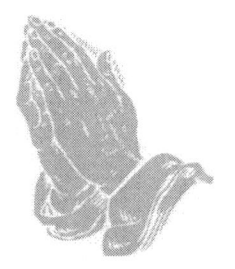

DAY 65

Prayer Focus: Peace
Scripture Focus: Psalms 56:3; Isaiah 26:3

Heavenly Father, whenever I am confronted with an issue that causes me to be anxious, I will choose to trust in You. Thank You for the perfect peace that only you can give.

Confession: I have peace that is not moved by circumstances.

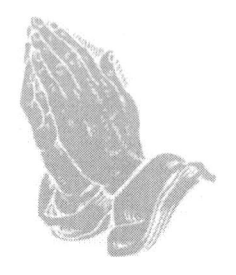

DAY 66

Prayer Focus: Victory
Scripture Focus: Romans 8:28

Heavenly Father, You are limitless and nothing is too hard for you. Thank You that you work things for my good when they are designed to destroy me. Only you can bring good out of chaos.

Confession: God makes me victorious in all situations.

DAY 67

Prayer Focus: Faith for the Future
Scripture Focus: Isaiah 61:7

Dear lord, for the many times I have endured the shame of invisible distress and pain, you relieve it with your promise of double joy! Thank you.

Confession: My shame does not go unnoticed by God.

<u>DAY 68</u>

Prayer Focus: A Proper View of God
Scripture Focus: Isaiah 6:1

Lord help me to never try to keep you at the level I am physically but enable me to lift you higher so you may draw me and others to you.. It is so.

Confession: There is a living God bigger than me.

DAY 69

Prayer Focus: I Cannot Grow Stronger by Myself
Scripture Focus: James 4:7

Merciful Saviour, my strength is being consumed and the enemy seems to be getting the upper hand. Help me to gain strength from the inside out.

Confession: Our togetherness is stronger than the enemy's temptation.

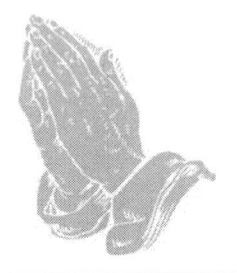

DAY 70

Prayer Focus: Overcoming Being Wounded
Scripture Focus: Psalms 147:3

Precious Master, here I am broken hearted and wounded. There is no earthly technology or medication that is positively healing me. Grant me prevailing grace for today with expectations for tomorrow. Amen

Confession: Even if no medicine can heal me, God can!

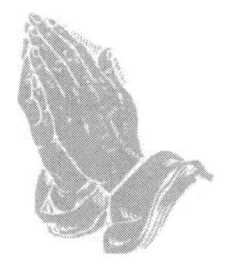

DAY 71

Prayer Focus: Finding a Large Miracle in a Small Situation
Scripture Focus: John 6:9

Loyal and Loving God, my progress seems so small in comparison to my diagnosis. Please give me insight in Jesus Name.

Confession: I am glad that God doesn't see things like I do.

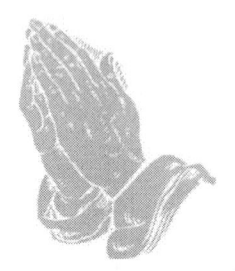

DAY 72

Prayer Focus: Sharing
Scripture Focus: Proverbs 19:17

Father, help me to be sensitive and generous to all but especially the poor, the needy, the marginalized, the homeless and the less fortunate. They could be me. In Jesus Name I pray.

Confession: My resources may not be the best but I am confident they are not the worst, so I can help others.

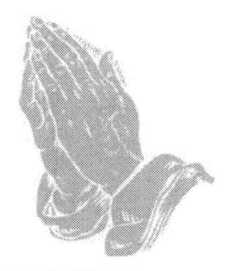

DAY 73

Prayer Focus: Understanding
Scripture Focus: Proverbs 4:7

Generous God, I need wisdom with understanding every day. Thank you for today's allotted portion and prompt me all day not to squander it.

Confession: God's simple way is better than man's complex theories.

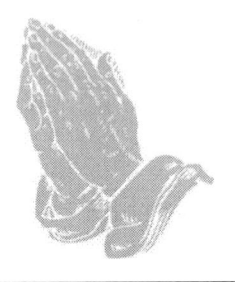

DAY 74

Prayer Focus: Knowing God Really Cares
Scripture Focus: Mathew 6:30

God of the Angel Armies, my heart leaps forth with great joy and excitement because your love for me dissolves the multitude of human oppositions and causes my spirit to smile. Amen

Confession: God you are aware of and care for everything you created! Hallelujah!

DAY 75

Prayer Focus: Being a Servant of the KING.
Scripture Focus: John 6:9

LORD OF LORDS, your presence in my life gives me the opportunity to be a blessing to others. Please use me to distribute your presence to others by my actions, in Jesus name I pray.

Confession: My servanthood to God brings blessings to my life.

DAY 76

Prayer Focus: Universal Beauty
Scripture Focus: Psalms 8:3

My Creator, the moon breaks the darkness like a hammer and the shattered fragments of light breaks forth in the night as twinkling stars. How amazing and resourceful you are! Thank you for being sovereign.

Confession: God is the ultimate definition of beauty.

DAY 77

Prayer Focus: How I Overcame
Scripture Focus: 1 Peter 1: 18-19

My Redeemer, as lost as I was, I was also lost from myself, yet you redeemed me for your purpose and the wonderful plan you have for me. Thank you ten thousand times isn't enough but I will start. Thank you!

Confession: The top of my valley is the bottom of your mountain. I want to be where you are.

DAY 78

Prayer Focus: Today
Scripture Focus: Exodus 32:29a

Joy giving Jesus, Today, I was not healed but I certainly was helped. Today, hope replaced agony. Today, I could see the light at the end of the tunnel. Today, the fire of progression burns brightly. Today, life is more than an empty four letter word. Thank you for today. Amen

Confession: Today is ready cash, spend it wisely.

DAY 79

Prayer Focus: Family
Scripture Focus: Galatians 3:29

God of the past, present and the future, I pray you bless us to walk as a godly family, in love, in your favor and forgiving one another. Help us to be living examples as you cover us with the power of the Holy Spirit for your glory.

Confession: Please make my life bigger than me.

DAY 80

Prayer Focus: Family
Scripture Focus: Genesis 17:7

Gracious God, thank you for making us a family that prays together and a family that will stay together to conquer the land you have given us to possess. We come against generational curses and release generational blessings in our household and for generations to come, in the name of Jesus, Amen.

Confession: I am a courier of generational blessings.

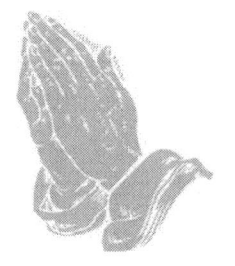

DAY 81

Prayer Focus: Family
Scripture Focus: Psalms 27:10

Everlasting God, I understand that one day my mother and father, through death, will leave me but even then you promised to be family for me. For this I am more than blessed. Amen.

Confession: God knows how to connect the dots.

DAY 82

Prayer Focus: Death
Scripture Focus: Proverbs 14:27; Psalms 23:4

Wonderful God, only your powerful love can bridge time and eternity; loss and gain; hurt and healing; emptiness and fulfilment; suffering and joy without redefining either. Thank you for being there for the defining moments of my life.

Confession: God is Sovereign and one of a kind.

DAY 83

Prayer Focus: No Condemnation
Scripture Focus: Romans 8:1

Lord, the enemy keeps bringing up my negative past and I don't feel forgiven. But thank you, it was your blood and not your feelings that did the work.

Confession: I am not perfect but I am forgiven and that sets me free.

DAY 84

Prayer Focus: Deliverance
Scripture Focus: Daniel 3:27

Christ of my salvation, you gave me deliverance from my fiery furnace experience not because of the absence of fear but because of my dependence on your presence. You did it again. Praise belongs to you. Amen

Confession: Faith is the launching pad for deliverance.

DAY 85

Prayer Focus: Bad News
Scripture Focus: 2 Kings 19:14

Lord, I refuse to let negative news that I can't change, change me so that I become negative. I place it before you and listen for your answer. Patiently I wait in Jesus name.

Confession: I cast my cares upon you for I know you care for me.

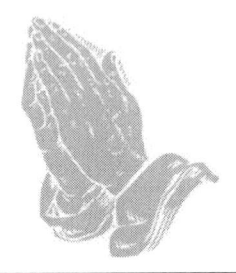

DAY 86

Prayer Focus: Prejudice
Scripture Focus: Acts 10:34

Merciful God, arrest my conclusions when I make final decisions about others with limited information or unilateral input. You still use flawed people, me included. Amen

Confession: We all came from dirt (the dust of the earth), so I will not judge.

DAY 87

Prayer Focus: My Thoughts
Scripture Focus: Philippians 4:8

Mind Regulating Master, from the waking moment of my eyes to last glimpse of light at night, let my thoughts be such that if displayed on a public screen they would not embarrass me nor you. In Jesus name, It is so.

Confession: I become my thoughts.

DAY 88

Prayer Focus: The Word
Scripture Focus: John 1:1; Proverbs 13:13

Eternal Father, the more I know your Word, the more I know You because You are your Word and your Word is You.

Confession: I find what I need in the Word.

DAY 89

Prayer Focus: Guarding My Mouth
Scripture Focus: Proverbs 13:3

Dear Jesus, encourage me through your Spirit to use my two ears, two eyes and two hands more than I use my one mouth. Forever I pray, amen.

Confession: Every discipline has its own reward.

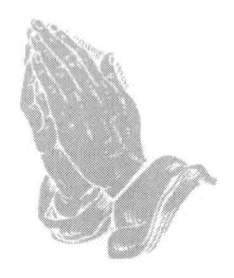

DAY 90

Prayer Focus: Affliction
Scripture Focus: Hebrews 11:25

Righteous God, if my choice is to suffer affliction with your people or enjoy sin for a season, I choose your people. Give me enduring mercy. Amen

Confession: Easy is not always right or the best.

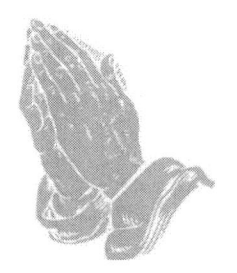

DAY 91

Prayer Focus: Being Diverted
Scripture Focus: 1 Kings 20:39-40

All seeing Father, keep me focused on my assignment so that I don't have to pay unnecessary penalties for being inattentive. In Jesus name I pray.

Confession: I must watch as well as pray.

__DAY 92__

Prayer Focus: Being Diverted
Scripture Focus: Luke 15:17

Generous Father, may the glitter of the world never draw me away from your wisdom and what you have for me.

Confession: I am not for sale because I have been bought with the blood of Jesus.

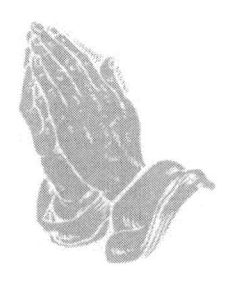

DAY 93

Prayer Focus: Status
Scripture Focus: Isaiah 42:6

Almighty God, I am grateful that you called me, hold my hand and keep me so that I reflect your light to the world.

Confession: My position in Christ explains my status in life.

DAY 94

Prayer Focus: Maturity
Scripture Focus: 1 Corinthians 13:11

Dear Father, direct me as I move from the easy liquids to more meats and solids in all areas of my life.

Confession: I need to transition from crawling to walking thou I run the risk of falling.

DAY 95

Prayer Focus: Power
Scripture Focus: Isaiah 40:29

Thank you dear God for granting me power when I was fainting and all but empty.

Confession: God promises me power at my weakest moment.

DAY 96

Prayer Focus: Victorious
Scripture Focus: 1 Corinthians 15:57

Everlasting Father, because of your Son Jesus, I praise you for permanently making me to triumph both in time and eternity.

Confession: I win with Jesus.

DAY 97

Prayer Focus: My Steps
Scripture Focus: Psalms 37:23

Lord, let me not be independent of you but inter-dependent on you.

Confession: I stumble less because my steps are ordered by God.

DAY 98

Prayer Focus: My Insurance
Scripture Focus: Psalm 37:23

Guiding God, I joyfully acknowledge that you cover your children with blankets of promises.

Confession: God has given the orders, I willingly obey.

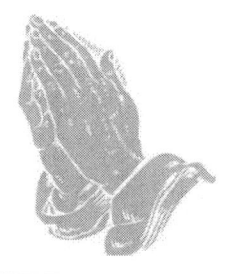

DAY 99

Prayer Focus: Maturing
Scripture Focus: Isaiah 54:2

Father of my life, in spite of my history or my present environment, I look to you as the expanding force in my future, knowing your plans for me will never fail. You deserve all the glory. Amen

Confession: I may fall but failure is not the design of my future.

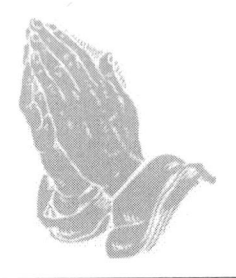

DAY 100

Prayer Focus: My Final Resolve
Scripture Focus: Proverbs 18:21, Romans 8:37

God, help me to know and acknowledge that I am who you say I am; the righteousness of you; the head and not the tail; more than a conqueror; a lender and not a borrower; loved and healed. Thus anything other than what you call me is an exaggerated fabrication from the enemy.

Confession: God is truth and He changes not!

ABOUT THE AUTHORS

Bishop George W. Brooks is Pastor Emeritus of Mount Zion Baptist Church of Greensboro, Inc. where he served faithfully as Chief Elder and Senior Pastor for 37 years. He also served for over ten years as Bishop of Administration of Full Gospel Baptist Church Fellowship, Inc.

Bishop Brooks holds a Bachelor of Science degree in Industrial Technology from North Carolina Agricultural and

Technical State University in Greensboro, North Carolina, a Master of Divinity degree from Shaw University in Raleigh, North Carolina, and Doctorate of Ministry degree from Friends International Christian University in Merced, California.

Bishop Brooks travels extensively speaking at conferences and revivals, and accepts other opportunities where he can proclaim the gospel. He endeavors to speak what the heart of God is saying to His people with relevance and clarity.

A believer in holistic ministry, he serves the community on a local, state and national level via Tri-State Christian Television (TCT) Board of Directors, Mechanics & Farmers Bank Board of Directors, North Carolina A&T State University College of Arts & Sciences Advisory Board, Beautiful Butterflies, Inc. (a nonprofit Lupus Foundation), and various advisory boards and boards of directors. Bishop Brooks was named among the "Most Influential Persons in the Triad" by The Business Journal from 2005-2012. Along with many other prestigous awards, he has also been granted the "Order of the Long Leaf Pine" given by the Governor of North Carolina and currently serves as the Suffragan Bishop of Global United Fellowship.

A native of Hillsborough (Orange County), North Carolina, Bishop Brooks is the son of the late Rev. Luther A. Brooks and Catherine Brooks. He and his wife, Edna, have two children and five grandchildren.

Lady Edna Brooks has had a unique walk and experience with God and has grown to love Him with her whole body, soul, and spirit. Having been healed by God at an early age of a brain tumor, Lady Brooks believes in the miraculous power of God.

For 37 years, Lady Brooks ministered to numerous adults and young people through teaching, leading people to Christ, and counseling with her husband who is currently the Pastor Emeritus of Mount Zion Baptist Church in Greensboro, North Carolina.

Lady Brooks received her Bachelor of Arts degree from North Carolina A&T State University and a Master of Religious Arts in Christian Psychology from Jacksonville Theological Seminary. She has attended numerous seminars and conferences, which has aided in her personal spiritual growth and is a member of the American Association of Christian Counselors (AACC). Prior to retirement, she served as Director of Encouragement at Mount Zion Baptist Church where she had oversight for eighteen (18) ministries.

Lady Brooks is the dedicated wife of Bishop George W. Brooks, mother of two children and five grandchildren.

As a motivational speaker and author, **Keva Brooks Napper** established MEEK LEGACY, LLC which educates and empowers others concerning invisible illnesses such as lupus. Keva has a Bachelor of Arts degree in Elementary Education with a minor in English. She is also the Founder and Executive Director of Beautiful Butterflies, Inc., a nonprofit lupus foundation. She teaches and facilitates groups as well as serves as an ambassador for Lupus Awareness through personal experience and pragmatic application.

Learn more about Keva at: www.mybeautifulbutterflies.com

As a family Bishop Brooks, Lady Edna, and Keva are believers in the power of prayer and its results. They seek the guidance of God through the study of his word, implementing of his commands and the acknowledgement of him as Lord and Master of their lives.

To contact the authors, email: kbnapper@gmail.com

Made in the USA
Charleston, SC
03 August 2016